SELF LOVE NOTES II

Affirming Poetry & Prose

ISBN 978-1957087023

 Published by Sunurchin

SELF LOVE NOTES II

Affirming Poetry & Prose

Michelle G. Stradford

DEAR READER

Welcome aboard the self-love journey! My hope is that the poems in *Self Love Notes: Affirming Poetry & Prose* will be a source of energy and light, a treasure trove of affirmations and meditations that you will continue to revisit until you discover the magnificence you have always possessed.

I like to think that our subconscious mind can become our superpower. We absorb the positive energy we are surrounded by and glow in the self-love we immerse ourselves in every day. We can grow self-love even stronger while our mind rests in a bed of uplifting seeds cultivated during sleep.

When searching for support, affirming words of encouragement, or an inspirational message, I hope you will turn to *Self Love Notes II* by reading a selection before you drift off to sleep or the moment you arise.

My greatest desire is that this book inspires you to move through each day with confidence, knowing that you are fully capable of living out your fullest potential.

Thank you for coming along with me on book two of my self -love journey!

Sincerely,
Michelle

DEDICATION

For every brave soul still learning to adore
(love, respect and admire) themselves.

Contents

It has long been proven
one thousand-fold
that life's most
precious element
is a well-nurtured soul.

Mine the hidden gold
laced into every tissue
of your loving, soft,
and malleable heart.

There, you will discover
an unlimited supply
of gilded wisdom
readily available
for you to draw upon.

Mine Your Gold

INSPIRE

I tied a protective bow
across my heart
as a reminder to heal
my faltered starts,
honor its sacred rhythm,
and celebrate
its unshakeable valor.

Yet, shielding me
from those who once
quickened my pulse
has shortened my breath,
depleted my strength
and disrupted my rhythm.

I finally discovered
that allowing others
to love the entirety of me
was all I ever needed
to fully recover.

Protective Bow

This pain will not become
venom on my tongue,
poisoning everything I taste,
putting at risk all I own,
making the bold choices
I dare to make feel wrong.

Even though I have been stung,
I heal the hurt with hope
until my high note is sung.

I pledge to shield my soul
from the bitter bite of life,
so my zest for living
reignites my internal fight,
growing me ever stronger.

At All Costs

Treasure the river
of life experience tears
you have cried.
It is expected, acceptable
and required
that you shed the shame
of all you have done
to survive.

Walk with your head
held steady and high
in deserved grace
as you determinedly stride
from your past in haste.
Sprint with everything
you have into
your abundant future.

Deserved Grace

While jumping headfirst
into the deep end
without knowing
how to swim
may appear reckless to some,
it requires repeated
leaps of faith,
unmatched levels of moxie,
and your own
unique blend of wild,
along with
an unrelenting credence
and a stockpile
of mistakes
before your dreams
will finally take.

Crazy Credence

Resilience is built
through challenge,
hardship, and repeatedly
being tested.

Strength is seldom gained
from continuing a struggle
that your heart
knows is futile.

You should emerge
from a tough experience
markedly stronger,
not irreparably damaged.

Exiting a treacherous path
that may prove harmful
is self-care in action.
Abandon the winless fight.

Self-Care in Action

Turning a blind eye,
by intentionally
closing your mind
to the fear facing you
or the threats
that almost slipped through
does not make them
any less dangerous.

Nor does it diminish
their impact
and capacity to harm you.
Listen to your instincts
and confront tough challenges.
Remain strong and vigilant
while you are honing
that positive mindset.

Vigilance

I am slightly bruised,
adept at bending,
but will never surrender
to breaking or pretending.

This latest life aggression
is nothing that a dose of steel
and a soft serving
of truth cannot heal.

Wrapping my worries
inside warm blanket folds
of self-kindness and hope
elevates my skills to cope.

Kind to Me

When you are constantly
at war with yourself,
inching ever closer
to the edge of destruction,
make the hard choice
to wave the white flag.

Sometimes,
fully surrendering,
then starting again
is the most courageous
decision you can make.

Courageous Surrender

I will set a torch
to vital bridges
if crossing them threatens
to do irreparable
harm to me.

I have nurtured
supportive relationships,
attained valuable knowledge,
and will use my talent
to build new ones
if required.

I will ascend above,
crawl beneath
or charge through
every obstacle
to complete my journey
and secure all that
is intended for me.

Torch Bridges

If constant overthinking
overwhelms you
or creates
waves of worry,
pause and focus
that thoughtful energy
on just one of your senses
for thirty minutes.

Then revel in the serenity
that returns to you.
Though the stillness
may prove to be fleeting,
calming thoughts
will soothe your neurons
and hold you
deep in healing.

Keep repeating those
clarifying visualizations
and intensify
your deep breathing
until tranquility comes
to claim you.

Return to Serenity

I am no longer
fearful of falling
down, back or apart.
I am ready to ride
uncertainty into the ground,
make enormous leaps
and break me open
rather than go on
thrashing around,
lost in life's ocean.

I will not meander
without purpose
through this world,
never risking enough
to encounter
crippling chasms
or uplifting pinnacles__,
all of humankind's
sentient experiences.
I was born to live
my birthright's highest.

Pinnacles

It's your heart for me.
It beats in the moments
you show up for,
feeds the faith you pray for,
creates the future you hope for,
expresses the love you long for,
and treasures the people
you take risks for.

Even if you cannot
see it now,
you are loved and adored
by friends and family,
even secretly by a frenemy.

If ever you falter,
know that you make
differences in lives
and are worth fighting for.
From life's mistakes,
there is no need to hide.
Never give up on you
or that passionate energy
powering your mystic aura.

Passionate Energy

You cannot begin
to know the depths
of your resilience
until you have crawled
across the rugged valley,
then clawed your way back
after being struck
by a ruthless adversary.

You are far stronger
than you have imagined.
Never underestimate
your capacity to battle
your fiercest enemy
then soar high
despite the damage
sustained by your wings.

Soar Steadily

Your inviting smile
puts the world on notice
that your life
is enriched with purpose.

Your trustful eyes
are an intriguing portal
to life's greatest
jewels of wisdom.

Your innate beauty
is incomparable.
That effortless grace,
just heart-arresting
and indelible.

I know that you
often grow tired
and believe your effort
goes unnoticed.

Promise to never stop
living for you
and allowing your sun
to filter through
the world's sadness.

You Matter

I made a pledge
to myself
that those berating words
I mumble beneath
exasperated breath
will never inhibit
or keep me
from believing
in my inherent worth.

At every turn,
I will transform
the nervous energy
from the deluge
of my negative thoughts
into motivating,
creative currency
that moves me
into a high state
of self-love positivity.

Infinite Worth

Just look at you!
All your warmth within
brightens the sky for days,
and chases darkness
from every room you enter.

Despite the clouds
eclipsing your eyes,
your radiant inner beauty
still wins and shines.

We can talk and cry
until all your tears dry
and the hurt subsides.
With me, my friend,
there is nothing to hide.

You never need
to pretend you're okay
when life is just not
turning out your way.

If that is not enough
for you to smile again,
then rest your head
on my shoulder.
I will always be here
to lift you up
and carry you over.

Nothing to Hide

Sitting with yourself
in reflective silence
is your most powerful
self-discovery practice.

While there, you can
open the hidden portal
where you stored away
your backup generator
charged with
illuminating your life's
most intriguing mysteries.

Sit with Silence

I pause to breath in
the rejuvenating vapors
of freshly poured
possibilities.

This blue day is dawning
into promises
of ochre sun rays
and golden tomorrows.

I'm igniting my palette
with electrifying colors
lighting the way
to my bold future.

Colorful Future

I drifted on buoyant waves,
swallowed salty nightmares
and awoke to seagulls
cawing a familiar song,
singing the demise
of my drowning dreams
to an unfazed world.

I capsized but somehow
survived the undertow
and washed to shore.
Here I stand again,
prepared to swim
once more against the tide.
I will breathe in
the seafoam spray
and fight off anything
that obstructs my way.

This exposed skin
has grown tougher still
and my conscious
is freshly cleansed
by oceans of prayers.
I am readied
with unshaken tenacity
to go at life again.

Unshaken

I commit
to living
full out,
astonishing the world
with unrelenting
bold acts
of courage
in bursts
of red fervor
that stun
and neutralize
my fiercest
competitor,
while inciting
creative
revolutions.

My Red Fervor

Resist becoming
intimidated
by haughty words
frothing from the mouths
of the untested and untried
who have never attempted,
let alone achieved
all the things
you have accomplished.

When you have feared the fire,
felt the burn, then walked
through it anyway
and emerged on the other side,
charred, but still standing,
it is easy to deflect
the negative shade cast
by dismissive onlookers.

You are the embodiment
of courage.
Stand tall in your moment.

Embodiment of Courage

Upon widening my view,
I have stretched,
evolved and witnessed
positive changes
infuse into and move me.
My vision is vastly improved
and is nearing perfection.

I am ever more empowered,
as I prepare to wholly own
life's tough decisions
now that I have witnessed
my own complexities
from disparate positions.

Near Perfection

If you are hating on yourself
because you are not yet
doing the things
that are the most compelling
or focused on the goals
you know you've been
put on Earth to do,
take one positive step,
even if it is simply
telling someone new
about your deep-rooted passion.

Write out your intention
so, it can evolve into something
that spins you into a frenzy,
consumes every ounce
of mental energy
until you feel spent
and deliriously complete.

Then just make one move
in your intended direction.
The tiniest steps
are the hardest to take.
Stand tall with pride
for any progress you make.

Intended Direction

The seeds of self-love
were planted deep enough
to protect my soul
from the cruel
and the weak.

Though my growth
may never be perfected,
I am learning
to embrace both my flaws
and humble talents
and to fully accept
my insecure frailties
and gallant virtues.

My evolution
is a delightfully messy
private revolution.

Private Revolution

Wait not for perfect moments,
favorable temperatures
or rainbow skies
painted in melted crayons.
Leap heart first into life,
ascending beyond
your visible boundaries.

Skydive into your future
with a wild uncharted mind.
Your ambitions are meant
to disobey rules that constrict,
confine and just don't fit.
Liftoff and transcend time.
Defy all mind-numbing logic,
any weight of gravity
that restrains your body
or imprisons free thought.

Let go of the worry
of taking a wrong turn.
Stop waiting for
a high wind to launch.
Take that chance on you
and surge through
your no-fly restrictive zones.
Your stubborn will
and an inspiring hunch
will lift you into flight.

Defy Your Gravity

You are a surging force,
infusing energy
into all you touch.
You pour more value
back into the galaxy
than you ever
extract from it.

You are remarkable!
Accept your accolades
as a proud woman
born of raw talent
and intrinsic humility.

Surging Energy

Before you set out
into the vast unknown
in search of knowledge
and riches untold,
try cultivating the treasures
within your control.

All those precious gems
residing in you,
that grace and strength
you stoically imbue
were hard formed,
meticulously polished,
shaped and toned
through years of struggle.

They have been waiting
patiently to be harvested
to usher you into
your growth season.

Your Gems

There are days when
you just wake up raw.
Emotions rip and roar
through your mind
like the edge
of a jagged saw.
Make sure to be extra kind
to those graciously
trying to support you.

Above all, remember
to use a gentle touch
with yourself
when your struggles
make you think
you are not enough
torching your last reserve
of mental clarity
and physical energy.

Gentle Touch

I am continually reaching
for my inner child
because her untamed
innocence
holds profound lessons
to teach me.

Her exuberance
for life funnels hope
into all I see.
Her bright eyes
wide with enthusiasm
keep my soul from crying
whenever I get lost.

Inner Child

If who you believed
you might have become
is vastly different from
your present persona,
it is time to launch
a personal renaissance.

A full-life makeover
and soul-stopping takeover
are possible if your drive
is fiercer than most
and your wild dreams
are colossal enough.

Wild Dreams

Make certain that
the boundaries
you negotiate,
and the necessary rules
you carefully create
to protect yourself
don't imprison you inside
an echo chamber.

Leave enough room
for fresh ideas
to take root in your head
and fully germinate.
Stay open to differing
viewpoints and listen
to external input.

Allow random thoughts
to circulate freely
and moments of clarity
to help you see your impact
on the world more clearly.

Echo Chamber

I am immensely proud
of myself for doing
what was required of me
to face and overcome
adversities.

I struggled my way
from the darkest side
of life's harsh realities
and refuse to hold
shame in that.

The battles I encounter
may never end,
but whether I lose or win,
I will consistently
show up for myself.

Self-Pride

You showed up,
yet tremble still
in the presence
of a chained door,
unmovable mountain
or treacherous enemy.

First frightened
motionless,
then beckoned to run,
you step forward,
walking boldly
into the fear.

Despite your tears,
you summon the courage
and wage a valiant fight
for your life.
You possess strength
far beyond your years.

Evidence of Courage

For just one day,
resist the need to fix
everyone or direct
and guide all things.
Try to relinquish
your perceived control.

Grant yourself
the devoted attention
and much-needed rest
that's deserving of your
weary soul.

Trust that the universe
will define the order
of your life
as it is intended
to unfold.

Unfolding

Even when you feel
uncertain
and the future
looks rainy-day murky,
turn the lessons
from that last misstep
into your life's
tremendous success.

The more significant
obstacles you face,
the stronger your ability
and the further humbling
is your grace.
The more often you fail,
the higher your trajectory
becomes to prevail.

High Trajectory

I stake bold claims
on my
transformative abilities
by doing one task per day
that builds
a reliable pathway
to achieve the bold,
life-affirming goals
that I hold
for myself.

I make the time
to move
my mountains,
one tiny triumph
at a time.

Pathways

I ended the wailing
over my broken parts
that have long
crumbled away
and the crippling pain
of a heart in decay.

I allowed the rain
to wash away
the tear stains
of my dismay
over the people who
consistently placed me
in harm's way.

I am leaving
it all behind
and focusing instead
with all my mind
on a place enriched
with simpler good times.

My less cluttered life
will leave room to build
better memories
and a future
filled with fortune
and positive promise.

Brighter Road

I will not become
a helpless victim
who assigns
my condition
to the actions
and decisions
of another human.

That which occurred
before today
is cast in the past.
I have done the work
to heal, recover
and get back on track.

My singular focus
drives the trajectory
of my unchartered future
into next-level
success.

Next Level

Remain avidly loyal
to yourself.
Fortify your unwavering
tenacity,
in the face
of attempts to undermine
your faith
in your convictions,
and any efforts to break
you down
by subverting
your self-confidence.

Avid Loyalty

Grant yourself permission
to be delighted
with the splendid you
that woke up today.
Your mental health
is vital to your well-being,
just as your physical condition
is important to upholding
your high esteem.

But while you are busy
retooling and investing
in yourself
with the latest
self-improvements,
be especially kind
to that vulnerable person
smiling back at you.

You may not yet
fit into the perfect red dress
or those shapely jeans
but you are still
a stunningly
gorgeous person.

You Are Gorgeous

She never leaves
a moment idle
for evil to sneak in
or a door closed
to allow regret
to lurk behind.

She fills her life up
with engaging souls
and breathtaking adventures
that sustain her joy
and generate
her happiest experiences.

Sustained Joy

Your quiet strength
is far stronger than
any disaster that threatens
to overtake you.

Resist those tears
and throttle any panic
that may stifle
your commitment.

Draw upon your
unwavering resolve
and steady yourself.
Just hold firmly
to your center
until the darkness
has passed.

Resist the Tears

Feeling incomplete?
Rediscover a passion
that stirs up your emotions,
gets you up on your feet,
and has a positive impact
on someone in need.

Plant inspirational seeds
that in time will grow
with your nurturing care
into relief and hope.
Greet each glorious sunrise
with a personal promise
to live in your purpose.

Lived Purpose

Repair your tiny cracks
to prevent precious energy
from escaping through
the most vulnerable gaps.

Cast aside all shame
or guilt that refuses
to loosen its grip.

Reject the negative lows
that threaten to rain
on your vibe and flow.

Vulnerable Gaps

The morning glistens
in fresh iridescent dew,
holding today's
abundant
promises for you.

Faint rays of sun
barely filter through
those clouds in your eyes,
yet you continue to show up,
though you want to hide.

The stage is set
for a day of beauty.
All that is required of you
is to free yourself
and allow your heart
to roam freely.

Day of Beauty

Sometimes my soul
sends me off to places
where I just need
to roam alone
to rediscover experiences
I forgot I had owned.

Whenever I return,
invariably I am carrying
a newfound part of my heart
that had been
hidden carefully away
until it was ready
to be retrieved
and put on display.

Although I may never
recover all that I have lost,
today I am closer
to being complete.

Rediscovering Me

You forged your way
through grueling challenges
to the other side
and fought through
waves of evil
that were freshly spawn.

After conquering them all,
you pulled those
who were lost,
but deserving into the light.

Take the credit
you are allotted
for earning your place
as a gallant enabler.

Rise up, stand tall,
and graciously take a bow.
You have worked diligently.
Your time is now!

Your Time

No more shrinking
me down
to avoid being seen
apart from the crowd
or to fit in to
that diminutive cage
intended to contain me.

My arms are stretched
as wide as
they can reach.
I've got a jubilant skip
in my heartbeat
and a roaring fire lit
beneath these restless feet.

I refuse to hear
any further no's,
so I look past
the disapproval glances
from my friends and foes.
I can no longer quell
my swelling pride.

Upon learning
to stare down the fear,
I am taking up wide
and tall spaces
to boldly show
that I have always belonged
in remarkable places.

No Shrinking

I have been long told
that in the boundless sky,
there are no limits to hold
me in captivity,
deny possibilities or shield me
from gravity.

I am igniting my rockets
to light up the night,
reach my targets
and prove them right.
I was born ready to fly
and fully own
this voyage of my life.

This Voyage

There may come a time
when the people you love
have strayed so far
away from the magical
connection you once shared
that they can
no longer be reached,
making you feel
incapable of giving
or receiving the care
you each needed.

Though the isolation hurts,
remember that you possess
everything within you
to see you through
this suffocating ache.
Self-love
is a soul-sustainer.

Soul-Sustaining

Despite how well you hide
from life's grittiness,
it finds and tests your strength
with unrelenting
persistence.

Remain firm in your
unflinching resolve,
because you have already
answered the call,
and more than proved
your fearlessness.

Unflinching

Never permit
anyone to limit
your perspective
or make you feel small,
objectified or subjected.
No one can define
how tall
your stature in life
will be but you.

Believe in yourself,
in all that is uniquely
your aura and truth.
Live your largest
each day to manifest
your upward
trajectory.

Largest Life

Take a seat and settle
into your thoughts
beneath the azure sky.
Tune your volume
up to a receptive high.
Soothe your scars,
and ignore those lies
about choices and regret
you have been taught.

Cradle yourself
in the arms of quiet
shielded from purpose
or whispers of time.
Listen raptly to the longings
you have feared
to utter aloud.

Your heart is worthy
of your intense affection.
Your time to feel deeply
is long overdue.
Indulge in a dream,
then dwell a spell longer
in all the wonder
that lives within you.

Be Heard

When giving love
unconditionally,
you expect nothing
in return.
This does not mean
you are willing
to sacrifice yourself
to be used up
and burned.

Do Not Sacrifice

Skin to skin touch
is an astonishing healer.
As the body's largest organ,
it is sensitive and revealing
with a direct pathway
to wherever the need.

Embrace someone
in a long body hug
or hold their palm
in a gentle caress
for a sentient moment.

Then feel the wonder
of human chemistry
work its intimate alchemy
to energize your bodies
and infuse your spirit
with delight.

Skin to Skin

To get out of your own way,
discover and capture
unpromised moments
by awakening
on a sun-filled day
with no defined plans.

Take a bike ride beneath
the shade of a grove
of majestic live oak trees
adorned in gray moss.
Listen as the passing breeze
whispers of the epic history
they have witnessed.

Share endless laughs
with a longtime friend
until you collapse
in teary-eyed grins,
while you hysterically
slap your knees in delight.

Search for backyard treasures
with a high energy child
or a languid adult
who has forgotten
the pleasure of fun.

When your day is done,
revel in the orange shimmer
of the evening sun
while licking a melting
sherbet ice cream cone.

Catch a moment of quietude
for yourself and reflect,
remembering a time
when life stood still
and simply being you
felt so good.

No matter what you've
chosen to be or do
on this unscripted day,
your delighted spirit
is sure to find
its way back to you.

Unscripted Day

This day felt unusual.
The river's current
had shifted anew.
A message for her was painted
across the sky in ribbons of blue
as the crisp air hummed
melodies of her long
awaited promises.

She could finally hear
the hope long lost
to her voice of reason.
She stepped out of the past,
arriving in the dawn
of tomorrow:
the commencement
of a new life,
and the end to her sorrows.

The Commencement

I have long endured
all the negative noises
from contorted faces
and the distracting forces,
pulling me into dark places,
clawing at my arms,
causing lasting harm,
and at times completely
knocking me to the ground.

I have been summarily
brought to my knees,
but this buckling
is purely temporary.

It won't be long
until I seize all I need.
But, oh, when I finally
break free, there will be
no one who possesses
the power to stop me.

No Stopping Me

MY SELF LOVE NOTES

IMPERFECT

Refrain from emptying
the entirety of yourself
into those who
are always demanding,
take instead of giving,
rarely understanding
and could care less
about you.

You may risk becoming
so enfolded
into their lives
that the essence of you
fades to invisible.

Reserve your sacred
energy for those
truly in need.
Avoid perpetual users
and generosity abusers
by setting and enforcing
self-protective limits.

Set Limits

Asking for assistance
whenever I need it
does not render me weak.
First acknowledging,
and then tending
to my vulnerabilities
significantly
strengthens me.

Strengthening

Be mindful of who
you invite into
your inner sanctum.
Their seemingly
harmless presence
and influence
may unhinge havoc
so stealthily
that you wake up
bewildered
of how and when
you were robbed
of your high esteem.

Protect Your Sanctum

Never tolerate
the negativity
of fringe friends
who constantly drain
your essential energy,
simply because
they fill up the voids
that you are unable
to face alone.

Instead, own up
to the reasons why
living in your blank spaces
blinds you in a blur
of stir-crazy,
making you feel uneasy
and uncomfortable
in your own skin.

Fringe Friends

You may call me out
as "overly controlling"
or "too strong" of a woman.

Either way, if you
are so easily intimidated
by my self-assuredness
and spirited energy,
you were never intended
to run with me.

Spirited

At times, you feel
trapped between
inherent self-trust
and not knowing enough.
Your suspended belief
prevents you
from stepping up.

Forgive yourself
for the opportunities
never taken
and the good fortune
you may have forsaken.

You were simply
not ready yet.
Vow to be okay
with that
and shower
abundant kindness
upon yourself.

Forgive Yourself

Despite
how magnificent,
selfless, loving
or respectful you appear,
not everyone
will connect with,
like or hold you dear.

It may not be about you,
but them.

You were never
intended to become
everyone's best friend.
Try to accept this reality
and uplift the ones
who consider you special.
Focus your efforts
on showing them
how much you value
their presence.

Not About You

I am grateful
to have emerged
from intense battles
that should have
destroyed and left me
writhing in tatters.

Yet sometimes I want
to shed my strong suit
and be swaddled
in a soothing blanket.
The resilient ones
grow weary too.

Strong Suit

If you often disappear
within yourself,
or isolate your heart
with miles of distance
to avoid engaging
with the people who love
and need you most,
you may have become
a self-saboteur
and an enabler
of whatever fear
that has taken
possession of you.

Take a cleansing breath
and deep dive beneath
your rawest emotions
long enough to isolate
the source of anguish,
then slowly rise
to the surface,
easing back
into your feelings
until you face down
one agitation at a time.

Face Down

Take note of the things
they refused to say
that should have been
uttered yesterday.

Hidden intentions
cloaked inside
of empty subtleties
and feelings shuttered
amid the storm
can be foreboding
of dark days to come.

The words withheld
are the most telling.
Listen intently.

Shuttered Feelings

It is long past the time
to break free
and toss away
the stained receipts
and bad scripts
of toxic relationships.

You are not a relic.

Trash that faded
playbook
so that you
can avoid traveling back
to that cyclical path
of destructive history.

Not a Relic

At times you must
choke down the bitter taste
after being served up
a cold plate
of distasteful
unfounded accusations.

All you are left to do
is to hold your nose
and swallow someone's
half-baked untruth.

Then, you pray incessantly
that their bullshit
does not get lodged
deep in your DNA
before you can filter
and expel it in nature's
intended way.

Bitter Taste

I unraveled
my contorted knots
one at a time,
disconnecting
the perplexing locks
that had tethered me.

I am no longer tied down
to someone else's boat,
their self-absorbed hopes
or the presumed
expectations of what
I should or could be.

I carefully pulled away,
discarding the tangled ropes
that were constraining
the made-up she.

Finally, I am free
to design the *real* me.
I stand ready to set sail
of my own accord
in my new custom-made
unmoored vessel.

Custom Made

You have ambled
down the road into a life
you never intended to lead.
You're trapped in a world
that makes you
feel lost and wounded,
even though you had once
believed it to be
all you ever needed.

Summon your instinct
to find your way out.
Turn around
and change your direction,
then go rebuild
a custom-designed future
that will finally
set your world right.

Summon Your Instinct

Bidding you hollow
well wishes
after politely escorting you
out the back door of her life,
she shoved
her purple bridesmaid's dress
back into your hands
on the eve
of your wedding day.

It is acceptable
to abandon the hull
of a friendship
that is already vanishing
amidst the murky mutterings
of the devout
yet unforgiving voice
who is intolerant of your
personal choices.

Abandon the Hull

I reject negativity
and will swiftly
jettison
deceptive people
who attempt
to subvert
my wellbeing.

There is no place
for you in my life
if manipulative
behaviors
and deceptive values
are what you savor.

My Boundaries

Choosing harmony
over stress-filled drama
has been freeing.

Unless someone's life
depends upon me,
I no longer insist on leading.

I now breathe easier,
relieved to have released
the need to be right.

Choose Harmony

I will not be unnerved
by the naysayers.
Their negative banter
shall never prevent me
from attaining my dreams.

They cannot inhibit me
from believing in the unseen.
Those yet-to-be realized
investments in myself
will eventually yield
lifelong dividends.

My distractors are resentful
of what I have accomplished,
the things I've overcome
and the amazing person
I have already become.

The envious have been toppled.
They are held suspended
in fear of this
unstoppable potential.
I am limitless.

Limitless

Your naïveté can be
a remarkable strength
if it emboldens you
to take daring risks
and embrace things
that the more enlightened
would never have
the courage to.

Do not consent
to anyone's attempt
to shame you
for not having had
the advantage
of knowledge.

Sometimes, the less
informed you are,
the more fantastical
your creative prowess.

Flex Your Naïveté

Some continue to dream
of being rescued
by a prince
from a life
of scrubbing floors
on their knees,
while others
march through the gates
and retrieve
what they need
without fitting
into a would-be savior's
magic shoes.

Success Tales

There were times in life
when she made poor decisions
by foolishly traveling
in the opposite direction,
and brashly turning away
from the easy choices.

She consistently
chose dereliction,
wrecking her own world.
She ran away from
the insistent desires
her heart was beckoning.

Yet, remarkably, life led her
to this amazing present,
granted untold experiences,
and molded her
into an unrelenting woman.

She is grateful
to have been shaped
into a magnificently melanated,
complex existence
with unmatched resolve
and tireless persistence.

Complex Woman

Fearlessness
is enabled in part
by ignorance.

Sometimes
knowing too much
can be a hindrance,
paralyzing
us into inaction.

Get on with it
and take a chance,
even if you don't have
all the answers.

Take Your Chance

The pain inflicted
by those who claim
to love me
cuts so much deeper
than the stabs
from the ones
who stand against me.

Betrayal cuts deeply,
knocking me to my knees
in a heart stopping
fetal position agony.

I am still learning
to hold my heart
as wide open as possible,
while still protecting
its fragile contents.

Deep Hurt

I am empowered
to make the brash moves
that drive my progress forward,
even when they result in
tough mistakes,
hard-earned lessons,
and regretful retakes.

I embrace smart risks
as I stand upon the shoulders
of family and friends,
confident in knowing
they will always
be there to catch me
in a judgment-free zone.

Judgement-Free

As I retrace my yesteryears,
I can scarcely see
the shadows that constantly
darkened my vision
or faintly hear
the doubt that once
questioned my wisdom.

I no longer feel the fear
tying knots in my fortitude
as I reach forward
to retrieve the life
that awaits me
in my future.

I have been transformed
into an unrecognizable
superhuman, a brute force
and unhinged fighter
ignited by unbridled passion
as I set my re-ignited
dreams afire.

Dreams Afire

When we lose ourselves
in our forest of fears,
it could take us weeks
to retrieve our soul
or even years
to find our way back
if navigating
the wilderness alone.

Take a pal
along on your
rediscovery journey.
A trusted companion
can keep us
from straying off
on to dangerous paths.

Close friends help us
count the stars
and collect the treasures
that have long
warmed our hearts
and kept the fire lit
in our eyes.

Rediscovery Journey

I ignored every single
nagging question
and the obvious lessons
until the injury
was undeniable.

In my quest to believe
in their best intentions,
I denied my heart
its emotions, stalling
with interventions.

My tongue became
tangled in the tension
of my conflicting thoughts,
silencing my voice
into submission.

I will never again
censor myself
to my own detriment.

Nagging Questions

She fixed her eyes
upon the luminary
she would soon become,
moving beyond the hollows
where she had begun.

She would never forget
the agonizing drought
from whence she had come.
But now she was powerfully
well-positioned.

Finally, she had overcome.

Well-Positioned

I spent too many years
lost between
the ebb and flow,
tip toeing over
someone else's insecurities
by disregarding what I know.

I was ardently
putting my heart's music
to other people's lyrics,
often believing I was choosing
what was in my best interest.

From today forward,
I am only living out the stories
belting the loudest notes
from my soul.
I will harken to that voice
beckoning me to soar.

If my spirit doesn't feel it,
I am done
and will just shut it down.
These songs that live
in my heart
will not steer me wrong.

Harken to the Voice

Solid decision-making
is a mindful process.
Never chastise yourself
for not knowing enough.

You will face thousands
of thought-provoking
questions
and life lessons.

It is okay to be at a loss
for answers.
Showing yourself
gentle compassion
is essential.

Gentle Compassion

You shall not invalidate
my feelings by dismissing
my sensitivities
as an overreaction.

Steer your passive-aggressive
words and abusive thoughts
away of me.

I own my emotions.
Please drive your baseless
points elsewhere.

Emotional Ownership

I no longer have reign over
the thirst for needing
or this drive to improve
every aspect of my being.
My greatest quest
is to see my goals
sprout in the wild.
Inspired, I am compelled
to scale my mountains
and face the frightening.

The fear of leaving
my dreams stranded here
without me seeing
them through
is an insistent drum
that drives me
to attempt things
others seldom fathom.

These ambitions
and so much more
direct and steer
my life ceaselessly.
I have no control over
this hunger that owns me.
My penchant for achieving
might someday
consume me...

Hunger Drives Me

There comes a time when
you must begin
to live better, eat healthier,
breathe easier,
forgive more readily,
and love with
unbound ferocity.

You will thank yourself
for the life-enhancing
and enduring
positive changes
that define the meaning
of authentic living.

Life-Enhancers

Your laughter wields magic.
It can banish storm clouds
from the edge of day,
shape smiles
from hardened clay,
and soften
the most cynical heart.

Someday you will
embrace your gift,
feel good in it,
and freely spread
the joys leaping high
in your spirit.

Your Gift

Consider daily stress
a necessary exercise
for your mental prowess.
Go on and flex
those mind muscles!

With the optimal strength
you are gaining,
you can better withstand
unconscious self-shaming
and resist taking on blame
by barely lifting a finger.

Mindful strength-building
is underrated.
You will never regret
growing a stronger
and more flexible mindset.

Mindful Strength

We are often too quick
to resent someone's behavior,
harsh comments or distance
when, in the end,
it is never about our failures.
Instead, it's a personal issue
the other person
may be facing.

Being closely attuned
to other people's needs,
hopes, dreams and wounds
can make us less defensive.

We become a better
brother's protector
or sister's keeper,
when we put in the effort
to understand someone's
concerns and unique
perspective.
Take your connections
a level deeper.

Attuned

Please do not assume
that I will tolerate
your attempt to test me.
You will never pierce
my stoic demeanor
and self-contained center.

My grace is hard-earned
through hell's storms,
destructive floods,
and life's many
adverse experiences.

I have long practiced
this piercing stare
and unyielding stance.
You are not talented
enough for this dance.

Stoic Demeanour

Never permit yourself
to be set on fire by someone
attempting to gaslight you.
Believe what you heard.

You cannot unsee
what was revealed to you.
Disallow anyone's effort
to convince you otherwise.

You are not overreacting,
nor are you unstable.
Their behavior is a blatant attempt
to manipulate you with lies.

Resist Gaslighting

When the disappointment
in herself had become
more damaging than
any criticizing words
or disapproving glances
from another person,
she set new standards
to which she held her life.

She removed the harsh rules,
hollow ambitions,
and self-inflicted pain
that were too dangerous
a price to pay
with her self-esteem.
Finally, she is flourishing!

New Standards

Showing up as a person
of great strength was never
my choice to make.

I instinctively took
the actions
that were required
of me to survive,
remain physically,
emotionally,
and mentally intact.

My intrinsic faith
and indomitable drive
kept me on track.

Person of Strength

Consistently being known
as the strongest one
or relied upon to always come
to the rescue of others
is not an invitation
to be taken advantage of.

You are not intended
to be everyone's
wonder woman.
Abdicate that flawed position
and focus your full attention
on your personal well-being.

Abdicate

You say that you would
like to truly know me,
but you can't make the time
to learn my history
or complete a conversation...

Despite how brilliantly
I paint my life story
with brushes dipped
in layers of poetry,
you never look beyond
my surface to understand
how deep my river flows,
or how much
my intuition knows.

It is a shame that you
are incapable
of fully recognizing
the tragedy
of this lost opportunity
and will never delight
in my most
glorious majesty.

Glorious Majesty

I have learned
in the cruelest way
that I cannot continue
giving the best parts
of me away
or risk my integrity
to entice people to stay.

I hope you choose
to embrace me,
not because you desire
something in return,
but because
you're compelled
by our shared alchemy.

Compelled

Those who insist
on tearing down
your ideas and dreams
and take pride in dismissing
your top accomplishments
with conniving schemes
and non-constructive criticisms,
may just be projecting
an adverse personal experience
from which they have
never recovered.

Deflect their venom
by turning the mirror around,
so their negativity can
reflect upon them.

Resist falling into the trap
of permitting another person's
unresolved issues
to become your
crippling crises.

Projecting

You are no longer in need
of fleeing from your worries
or allowing them
to reduce you to tears.

No more running
or being chased away
while screaming
through the wandering years
too frightened to dream!

Halt your retreating steps
and turn around.
Summon all your resolve
and stare the fear down
with newly hard-formed
steel steadying your eyes,
then return to creating
the life you deserve.

Steel in Your Eyes

I hope you recognize
that acting upon the advice
of someone who
is not required
to live with the consequences
of your life decisions
may prove unwise.

Be wary of seeking direction
from those with limited
perspective on your view.

Those who have yet
to navigate your path
or cannot empathize
with the conditions
unique to you
may not offer up
a sound solution.

Unwise

When your carefully-made
plans and brilliant ideas
keep missing the mark
time and again,
you may believe life itself
is conspiring to prevent
you from winning.

Perhaps it is time
to just tear it all down
and usher in a new day.
Implode those stubborn boulders
that are blocking your way.
Obliterate the giant obstacles
that have invaded your psyche.

Blast away anything
impeding your goals.
Start afresh and build anew
from the ground up
on a firmer foundation.

Your new concept,
bold construct
and ambitious goals
will offer greater possibilities
and stunning views
for a grander you.

Grander You

I rate the toxicity level
nesting inside people
with my shape shifter meter.
Then I eliminate them all
from any daily connections,
which makes my world
simpler and richer
with meaning.

Their impact on my life
no longer registers.
My body and mind
both thank me
for extending
our longevity.

Eliminate Toxicity

Granting someone access
to your intimate thoughts
and sharing your path
in life's precarious walk
is a privilege that is best
not treated casually.

Ensure the highest quality
in your connections
while trusting the shared values
and strong chemistry
in the bond you are building.

Be assured your chosen person
is the caliber of friend
that will stand with you
through fire and wind,
and is someone upon whom
you can always depend,
when life is not pretty
or your world is upended.

The Basis of Friendship

I feel a vibrant pulse
slicing through me
like a lightning rod,
electrifying the suffocating air
with heated energy.

My truth is so close
that I feel
the burning lies
crumbling into ash,
finally releasing me.

I fully acknowledge
my vulnerabilities
and accept
my imperfections
as a vital part
of my flawed beauty.

My Imperfections

Feeling trapped in her past,
she aggressively sought out
the lessons in her
most egregious mistakes
and released
any remaining regret
into the wide-open skies,
so it could dissipate
into the ether.

She watched all guilt
escape the atmosphere,
like rising crimson balloons
bursting in cold thin air.
She vowed to readily
forgive herself when making
the inevitable future stumbles.
The freedom to try again
was incredibly humbling,
edifying and hope filled.

Readily Forgive

When the people she admired,
and cared for could not feel
a shared connection with her,
she had to learn
not to take it so personally
and cease internalizing
their perspective
as rejection.

The damage to her self-esteem
was unsustainable.

She reclaimed her worth
and focused her efforts
on those who poured
their energy into her.
Learning that she
was appreciated
by a selective few
was a freeing realization.

Reclaimed Worth

Today I am picking up
where I stepped off
my transformation journey.
Growth is a never-ceasing
life continuum.
There will be
no turning back this time!

I will cease chastising myself
for breaking down
or falling apart.
All things that function well
must be properly
maintained and repaired.

I choose to get on
with making *me* happy,
by vaulting forward
with my life plan.

Vault Forward

She canvassed her situation.
The sun receded to the edge
of the melting sky.
She was ever-watchful
for when a cleansing
was required.

The darkness stormed in
and poured steadily for days,
ravaging her world.
She treaded water
for near an eternity.

Yet, in the aftermath,
both she and the blue sky
re-emerged ever-clearer.
Hopeful light finally reigned
over her world.
It was her time!

Her Time

Leaving behind
all I had known,
losing my way in life's
onslaught of storms
and unlearning the behaviors
that caused me harm
all led to me finally discovering
the tenacious being
I had long abandoned.

Today, I am grateful
to have reunited
with my fighting spirit.
I find comfort in knowing
that my most
loyal companion
has been waiting
patiently for me
to finally arrive.

Fighting Spirit

Michelle G. Stradford

MY SELF LOVE NOTES

GROW

Please do not become
so at home
inside the trappings
of your warm cocoon
that you cannot imagine
the possibility and beauty
that a life of freedom
has already spun for you.

Not all nests enable
growth and protection.
Some are dangerous
and unhealthy.
Knowing when to leave
a home, a person
or an entanglement is crucial.

Cocoon Trappings

I am done breathing life
into someone else's dream
while not investing
in the person
I am destined to become.

I will no longer
lose myself,
wasting
irreplaceable time
by existing in between.

My Destiny

Even though a stumble or two
may have slowed
life's frantic pace,
you will arrive
in good time
exactly where and when
you were intended.

Steer the navigation
of your journey.
This is no one else's race.
Resist cheating yourself
by attempting to exist
simultaneously
in multiple places.

Your Pace

The most important
relationship
you will ever need
is the one with yourself.

If you cannot be honest
in your beliefs,
swim in the deep
submerged in all your feelings,
face what you fear most,
and are unable to name
your ultimate desires,
you might be
unprepared to realize
all that's required
of your talents,
leaving your future
hanging in the balance.

You may be on a path
of sabotaging
the future you.

Future You

When you begin
to believe
you are failing
at everything,
the reason may be
that you have
stopped listening
to the needs
that your soul sings.

Those missed turns
and unattained goals
might just mean
that you have yet
to embark
on the right journey.

Soul Sings

I rush to fill my thirsty veins
from this new well
of abundance,
only to see my dreams
filter through the sieve
of my fingers
in all directions.

The shame that once
imprisoned me
is breaching
my containment walls,
spilling ceaselessly
into fresh reservoirs
of grace and acceptance.

Happy tears release me
as despair flows
unimpeded
out of my agitated crevices.
I am renewed,
slowly filling up
with unlimited promise.

Self-Acceptance

Although it initially hurt
to lose the support
of someone I believed
to be critically important,
not having them in my life
lightened a burden
I had not realized
that I had been carrying.

I often behold myself
to the wrong people.
Letting go of them
and their toxicity
was a huge relief
that proved uplifting
and restorative.

Wrong People

The moment I banned self-pity
from my vocabulary,
both shame and doubt
vanished from my psyche.

Putting myself down
is no longer a page I turn to.
Bullying behavior
is not my reality.

I am *new me* building
with encouraging thoughts
and forceful actions
that sustain and uplift me.

New Me Building

I lift my hands in surrender
and release all guilt
from the wrong choices,
poor decisions,
and shaky foundation
I have built.

I will make more mistakes
along life's journey.
I shall set aside my pride,
taste the bitter medicine,
and continue despite
the consequences.

Failure is a growth serum.

Growth Serum

I pledge to not use
words as weapons
against myself.

Whenever I make
a slight misstep,
forget something
meaningful
or do not possess
the right knowledge,
I will be kinder to myself,
offer an uplifting message
of encouragement,
whisper a silent mantra
of self-forgiveness
and move on.

Words can pierce deeply
and have lasting impact,
even the ones that are
mouthed in silence.

Word Weaponry

I embrace and own
my blunders.
But these mistakes
will never define me,
nor will they ever
prevent me from shining.

The misjudgments I make
do not confine me,
as I am constantly
learning and evolving.

Despite my shortcomings,
I am a responsible human.

Evolving

Do you understand
your core tenets?
Is your life's map
based upon an authentic
underlying premise?

Are you creating
a genuine original self
or simply curating,
assembling snippets,
and collecting fragments
of someone else's existence?

Are you fashioned
of borrowed high-gloss pages
from internet strangers?
Are you focused on editing,
retouching and applying filters
to enhance your many faces?

Do you subconsciously
embellish the details
of your life,
uncertain of what is real
or just another white lie?

You scroll past
hundreds of selfie
images each day,
unknowingly assuming
traits from others.

Are you the truth
or an excuse
of the authentic you?

Original Curation

I grimace and wince
whenever life's
sharp edges attempt
to sand down and cast away
my essential grit.

I keep a tiny collection
of grains in my shoe
that simultaneously agitates me
and pulls me through.
Their presence drives me
to operate with
full potency strength.

Essential Grit

Negative people may
desperately attempt
to throw shade on your vibe,
send your anxiety
into overdrive,
or cloud over
your sunny outlook
by brushing a fresh
coat of gray complaints
across your breakout day.

Have them leave
their muddy thoughts
outside the door
of your carefully-created
positive psyche,
prior to entering
your protective domain.

Your Domain

Desperate desires
often trick my eyes
into seeing,
and my head
into believing
the things I urgently
need to be true.

Taking a step back
and pausing
for a deep breath
helps me see my reality
more clearly,
and has accurately signaled
my new beginning.

Clear Signals

The thin layers of magnifiers
through which I now see
have made a key difference
in my innate ability
to recognize that despite
my claimed enlightenment,
much remains hidden.

There is so much more
to life, and to me
that's yet to be discovered
and to be made clearer
through my wider lens.

Wider Lens

Where would you be
if you stopped
opening yourself up
to just anyone?

What if you never again
were on the receiving end
of passive-aggressive
misogyny
from a man
or a woman?

How different
would your life be
if you more cautiously
granted your trust
to only those
who are truly deserving?

Proceed with Caution

Forgive yourself
for the self-directed
sabotage and aggressions,
failure to stand up
for your own cause,
and believing someone else's
assessment of your worth.

Make today the moment
you finally let go
of every self-righteous
or baseless excuse
that has denied you
of the care you need.

Stop saying no to you.
Seize every opportunity
to treat yourself
like the deserving
person that you are.

You Are Deserving

Upon finally forcing myself
to be honest enough
to name the behaviors
that were holding me back,
I discovered multiple doors
that I had never noticed
and was too paralyzed
to swing open.

I summoned my brave face
and turned the lock,
releasing myself
from wasting inside
my self-constructed prison.
I was shocked to discover
the pathway to the journey
I had long envisioned
had always been
within my power.

Power to Release

Meticulous
with your details,
you carefully deliberate
each tough decision,
calculating strategic moves
with focus and precision.

Your significant
life changes
are impactful
and your progress is real,
even as you move
at the speed of a glacier.

Progress Is Patient

I will conquer
today's mountain
by organizing
my larger-than-life dreams
into daily sprints.

My success will build
from micro-sized actions
that are easier to begin,
and will crescendo
into a dopamine-filled
spectacular finish.

Micro Actions

There is nothing worth
placing your sanity
at risk for.
Never question
your self-worth
when you falter.

Failing is essential
to your continued growth
and evolution
as an enlightened human.

Your hard-earned lessons
will strengthen
your mental acuity
and infinitely increase
your intrinsic value.

Self-Worth

Self Love Notes II

She listened to her psyche,
feeling anger rise
as it boiled over
in an enraged heat.
She refused to cool
or soothe herself
into submission.

She marched with
her hands raised,
white flag flying
into the ire,
and surrendered
to the fiery moment.

Into the Ire

The challenges and tests
that nearly broke me
have transformed my world
and developed me
into an inherently
stronger woman.

While my life's journey
has not always been easy,
by grace, a higher energy
delivered me.
For that, I am grateful.

Stronger Woman

Should you find yourself
on the precipice
of a breakthrough
and your need for space
to gain perspective,
clarity and a different view
is consistently ignored,
disengaging
from all that distracts you
may be a noble path
to personal freedom.

Path to Freedom

To calm my anxieties,
I cautiously move through
layers of complex emotions.

Uncovering my
stripped down raw self
must occur before
the real work on growth
can begin.

I pledge to remember
to treat myself
with exceptional care
until my self-love journey
is completed.

Complex Layers

Focusing on the possibilities
and building on
your potential
gives you less time
to retrace old missteps
or attempt to change
your past regrets.

Put those obsessive skills
to work by planning
your ideal future
in meticulous detail.

The Possible

You must first escape
the madness to comprehend
that you have
been held captive
on a path that
was unintended.

Take a mental break,
a thought-freeing sabbatical
so, you can
fully return
to rediscovering
your magic.

Only then will you recapture
the focus and clarity
you had been seeking,
and take a step
in the right direction.

First Escape

It was virtually
impossible for me to see
myself with clarity
with my mirror covered
in the false imagery
of perfection
I had painstakingly
created.

I thoroughly cleansed
my perspective
before attempting
deep-dive meditations
or self-reflections.
A clear view made
all the difference.

Reflections

List the mountains
you must move
to retrieve the treasures
intended for you.
Is your plan
to climb over
or tunnel through them?

Naming your obstacles,
whether imagined
or hard truths
is the first step
to pierce the sky
so that you can ascend
high enough
to retrieve your crown.

Move Mountains

Procrastination
is my burden.
Just as I get started,
my mind bends sideways,
traveling me down
unending rivulets
of overthinking loops.

At times, I believe
I have sunk to my lowest
and dry-drowned.
But somehow
I break the surface,
take a breath
and see that I caught
a rebound.

I offer myself
generous compassion
as I learn
to concentrate
on one path at a time.

Self-improvement Project

I am slowly becoming
more competent
in speaking up for my needs,
even when I feel threatened
or humility brings
me to my knees.

Self-confidence
is a survival trait I must
continue to strengthen.
I am responsible
for standing up for myself
and creating my own
happy existence.

Survival Trait

Try to breathe through
your rising anxiety
until it falls
and dissipates.

Acknowledge that
your trepidation is real,
then remind yourself
that you remain confident.
With thoughtful focus,
you will overcome it.

Fear cannot exist
unless you remain
an active participant
in enabling it.

Fear Dissipates

Your thorns know
their purpose.
They clearly understand
the primary assignment
to fend off all aggressors
attempting to harvest
your delicate petals.

Never apologize
for protecting
your seeds
so, they survive
life's challenges
and are preserved
to grow your future.

Thorns Know

The broken version of me
that grew to believe
something was wrong with me,
instinctively
shouldered the blame
for every mistake,
even the ones
others would make.

The healthier me
now owns up to my missteps,
takes responsibility
for only me,
makes the correction
and moves on.

Learning that I am not
the deep fault
triggering the tremors
that caused everyone's
world to shake
was the hard lesson
that freed me.

Healthy Version

There is nothing foolish
about occasionally
feeling inadequate.
Doing so is a natural
human condition.

You are expected
to have a wealth
of growing to do.
Avoid allowing
the thought of not achieving
all you desire
to stifle or limit you.

Instead, embrace
your weaknesses
or lack of knowledge
as a catalyst
and inspiration
to keep reaching higher.

Human Condition

Some days you must
fight even harder
to stave off the demons
that try to shape-shift you
into someone lost
and lacking sheer will,
which is an existence
and experience
completely different
from the fighter
you know yourself to be.

Keep pushing through it.
They can never break you
or breakthrough
your stone walls
cemented in self-love
and elevated on a platform
that you
stand firmly upon.

Sheer Will

Do everything in your power
to remain upright.
When challenges knock you down
for the thousandth time,
stay in and fight.

The change happening
each time you fail
is forging you
into a dangerous weapon.

Dangerous Weapon

She is slowly unwinding
her self-effacing habit
of apologizing first
before asking a question
or making a request.

Speaking with straightforward
intention requires
unwavering confidence
and consistent practice.

She is finally learning
that distinctly articulating
her views and needs
with clarity and ease
is an act of self-love.

Intentional Self-Love

When your apprehension
is whipsaw stressing
and stifling you
into inaction,
shut off the toxic noises,
the second-guessing voices,
and trust yourself again
with one
crucial decision.

Finding the courage
to make one small choice
is the first huge step
on the long path
of returning to yourself.

Small Decisions

Being chronically busy
was a convenient way
to camouflage and deny
the dysfunction
I worked to keep at bay.

Reality caught me
from behind,
disorienting
and slowing my grind.
Halted, I finally recognized
the path of destruction
upon which I had
been traveling.

I paused and did the work
to correct my course,
and now I am on my way
to a happier
and calmer existence.

Halted

Your growth has paused.
All self-development
is ebbing and slowing,
while your excuses
and imaginative reasons
continue growing.

Sit still with the behaviors
that have stalled you.
Only you can determine
whether you possess
the resolve to get unstuck
or allow fear to sink you
to your bottom.

You were not meant
to remain thwarted
and forever stunted.
Claw your way out.
Release that stunning
breakthrough
that you've been building
inside of you.

Stunning Breakthrough

Should my day spiral
dizzyingly out of control,
causing me to briefly
lose sight of my goals,
I will find my center
and remain mindful
that progress
seldom happens
the way I have imagined.

I am adaptable, pliable,
and a resourceful planner.
I will adjust, refocus,
and get back on the path
that I had been traveling.

Resourceful

There will come a day
when you can leap taller
than the height
of the walls you
carefully built
in your mind.

Developing your
mental prowess
and courage
requires time.

You will emerge
from the shadows,
overcome
your own barriers
and finally shine.

Emerge

She is unlearning
her people-pleasing
eagerness
to put the needs of others
always before hers,
lifting their goals in life
higher than her own
and putting them
atop a pedestal.

She was consistently
letting herself down.
Those days are over!
She is now raising
herself up first
to the highest pinnacle.

Raise Up

Pay attention to the things
you reluctantly do
that make you feel
either guilty or used.

Finally saying no
may be unsettling
and bruise someone
else's feelings,
but your newfound
liberation
will infuse you
with healthy energy
and positive self-esteem.

Healthy Energy

Keep that hope burning
brightly in your eyes.
You will melt away
the frosty blocks of ice
that preserved
your body and mind
while your world
was burning down.

This is your growing season.
Soon, the sweet fruits
of hurt and sacrifice
will be yours
for the keeping.

Growing Season

When feeling unwanted
triggers the most painful
bouts of rejection,
instead of immediately
launching into
self-improvement mode,
search within yourself
for the reasons
you consistently
attract people
who are unsuitable for you.

Negative experiences
are not always
about your inadequacy,
but may be due
to their insecurities
and hidden questions.
Assess whether the people
you invite into your life
truly measure up
to your expectations.

Measure Up

Sometimes, breaking
ourselves open
is the only way
to relieve
our ever-pressing pain
and empty longing.

I broke open a vessel
finally allowing
years of self-restraint
to free-flow.
The dormant danger
looms imminent.

My repressed ambitions
can no longer
be contained
in the face
of me over heating
and releasing
the truth
feeding this fire.

Relieve the Pain

It is okay to outgrow people.
Like ocean currents,
some relationships
ebb and flow,
first lifting you up
and then pulling you under.

Cautiously watch the riptide,
as some connections
can sink you so low
that the end for both of you
may prove to be inevitable.

Outgrowing

When I refused to wait
for inner calm
to balance and steady me,
reality snatched the wind
from beneath me.
My crash was destructive.
Self-care note:
slow down.

Rushing the process
and attempting
to outpace progress
without receiving
life's lessons
can prove to be
counterproductive.

Your enchanted life
will be waiting for you
when you finally arrive.

Slow Down

Before attempting
to become whole again,
by making critical changes
that are life altering
or struggling
to replace an element
you believe is missing,
look deeper into the chasm
and pierce through
the leathered layers
beneath your skin.

You may discover
that your vital parts
have gone into shock
and have retreated
to hide the bleeding.
Be mindful to first
understand the reason
that they fled
before attempting
to retrieve them.

Deep Exploration

This race with time
can break you,
and make it
nearly impossible
to finish anything.

It will siphon
your health and freedom,
make it difficult
to sustain your stability,
and challenge
your sanity
until you learn
to decelerate and replenish.

Whatever it is that
is driving you ragged
can wait.

It Can Wait

I refuse to allow
the chains of my past
to lock me out
of my future.

So, I capture
the hard lessons,
then block the door
to transgressions.

I am removing
all impediments
that no longer work
in my life.

Though frightening,
I welcome the uncertainty
that represents
the potential for a fully
illuminated life.

Uncertainty

It is okay to bask in
a *me day* to stitch
yourself back together
after a brutal yesterday
nearly broke you.

You may need heavy ropes
to lift and carry your
thin thread of hope,
or assistance with restraining
unhealthy thoughts,
by quieting the tantrums
stomping around
in your head.

But once you complete
the mending,
all that under-breath swearing
must be arrested,
for any further tearing
to be prevented.

Your Me Day

I deliberately shattered
all of my
perfect pictures,
then re-arranged
my broken pieces
into a life
that I had long
reached for.
I reframed a future
that makes me feel
even more beautiful.

Perfect Picture

MY SELF LOVE NOTES

FROM THE AUTHOR

I am grateful you completed reading *"Self Love Notes II."* I hope you found comfort, affinity, and inspiration in the poetry and prose.

Feedback, whether a phrase, a brief sentence or a paragraph, is valued and appreciated. Your input helps me validate my themes and informs me about what I should write next. So, please take a moment to leave a rating and review online at the retailer site where you purchased this book.

To stay updated on my next book release, read samples of work in progress, etc., please connect with me:

TikTok @michellestradford
Instagram @michellestradfordauthor
Twitter @mgstradford
Facebook @michellestradfordauthor
Pinterest @michellestradfordauthor
Bookbub: michelle-g-stradford
Goodreads: Michelle G Stradford

 Subscribe to my newsletter for book release updates, promotions, and giveaways by scanning code or search https://linktr.ee/michellestradford

I'm Rising: Determined. Confident. Powerful

Rise Unstoppable

I was broken
and tired of hiding,
when finally
I held up the mirror
to peer at my fractured parts,
and saw that
pain and struggle
had not twisted me
into something angry,
unrecognizable and hideous,
but into a courageous,
bolder, and more
formidable me.

Formidable

She tugged firmly
on a thin thread of faith
untied herself, just let go,
and released her fear of
unraveling.

She watched herself unspool,
her magic unfolding
into infinite potential.

Unravel

SCAN QR CODE TO GET A SIGNED COPY OF BOOK

ACKNOWLEDGMENTS

I offer my heartfelt thanks to my husband and daughters for their love and support. They breathe life into everything I do.
Thank you to my editor Eva Xan for pushing me to refine my words and sharpen my messages to create my readers' best experience.

And finally, thank you to the readers who continue to purchase and read my books. Those of you who reach out to share how my words have encouraged you or helped others keeps me going. I am grateful to each of you.

EXCERPTS FROM SELF LOVE COLLECTION

Self Love Notes: Uplifting Poetry,
Affirmations & Quotes

Self Love Notes II: Affirming
Poetry & Prose

Someday I will grow
brave enough
to carefully unfurl my secrets
and watch them free-fall
in velvet blankets,
like the petals of a rose
finally discovering
the beauty of freedom
now that they
are no longer trapped
inside the folds
of my soul.

My Secrets

You are far stronger
than you have imagined.
Never underestimate
your capacity to battle
your fiercest enemy
then soar high
despite the damage
sustained by your wings.

Soar Steadily

SCAN QR CODE TO GET A SIGNED COPY OF BOOK

ABOUT THE AUTHOR

Michelle G. Stradford is a bestselling Author, Architect, Artist, and Photographer who creates written, visual, and inhabitable art. Her writing style is contemporary free-verse, as her goal is to create poetry and prose that is relatable and inspiring to her readers. Besides poetry, she has authored short stories and fiction since adolescence.

Michelle strives to use her experiences and writing to build a platform encouraging women and girls to own their power, overcome challenges and attain their goals. She is married and has two daughters.

EXCERPTS FROM ROMANTIC COLLECTION

Waves of You: Love Poems

When Love Rises

Your love does not
take my breath away.
It breathes life into me,
no matter how high
you lift my soul
or how deep
you send me
searching.

Soul Search

I inhaled the breath
you exhaled
and in a singular moment
we breathed life
into this
extraordinary love.

Kissed to Life

SCAN QR CODE TO GET A SIGNED COPY OF BOOK

OTHER BOOKS

by Michelle G. Stradford

Inspirational Poetry

I'm Rising: Determined. Confident. Powerful.

Rise Unstoppable

Healing Grace: Inspirational Poetry for Coping & Closure

Self Love Notes: Uplifting Poetry, Affirmations & Quotes

Romantic Love Poetry

Waves of You: Love Poems

When Love Rises